Aquarium Heart

Jenny Prater

Print ISBN 978-1-952185-10-6
Digital ISBN 978-1-952185-11-3

Cover design and interior layout by Jenny Prater.

Wax Heart Press

waxheartpress.com
jennyprater.com

For friends who don't exist anymore—for the memories of people we used to be.

Contents:

Editor's Note:

Aquarium Heart includes the complete contents of Jenny Prater's now-out-of-print poetry collections *Goodbye and Other Words I Should Have Said* and *Avalanche: A Self Portrait in Verse*, as well as 66 new poems.

Acknowledgements

Special thanks to my supporters on Patreon: Jeff and Sue Prater, Lynn and Lowell Nystrom, Beth and Steve Cragle, Sam Medlock, and Jamie Krause!

Sad

These are the days you miss the mania
Days you stare into your pillbox and pause
Because it's a fifty-fifty shot
And you're already sad, so why not?
There's nothing to lose
Right?
Right?

It's a fifty-fifty shot
So maybe you'd still be sad
But maybe a handful of pills down the drain
Will give the soaring sort of joy
You haven't felt in so long
Maybe it's worth the chance to be happy,
Giddy and busy and never tired

You're always so alone, these days
And maybe manic, you wouldn't mind
Because manic, nothing matters
Except the next kind of fun you'll have

Nothing ever matters
But you miss the days that fact felt good
Before the pills took that magic happy away
And left you with routine sad

Medusa

A man hurt me
Now I hurt them
It's not revenge
It's self defense.

The serpents say forgive yourself
But there is no redemption
For weathered stone
And I live on this island alone
While you and your pickaxe are safe at home

I am a garden snake with venom
The frog that kisses back
I am new blue jeans
With holes in the knees
Stylishly broken
Messily clean
Always chipped and cracked
But crumbling, I'll take you too,
An avalanche

The You You Were

If I could go back—
I wouldn't
If I could see you again
The way you were then
Hair tangled, eyes smiling,
Muddy at the knees and elbows—
No, no, I wouldn't

You are perfect in my memories
And I hate you in present reality
I don't want to find
You were like this the whole time
Edges softened in my mind

Time machines are for someone braver

I wouldn't go back
To see the you you were again
I want to hold on
To my love for a you long gone
Can't risk learning that you
Was my own invention all along

Melting

My bones are made of ice.
I felt them freeze inside me long ago
That deep, deep cold when my skin is hot
And all that holds me up is frigid fear

I have been skin around a snowman for so long
I forgot to notice
How brittle I am and harsh and jagged at the edges
But now I notice, now
I feel the blood rush up and down my veins too warm

I wish
That you would press warm fingers to my wrist
And melt me into life again.
I have been so frozen and far away
And safe, but now is the time to thaw,
To be a puddle at your feet.

Aquarium

You are dried algae
On my aquarium heart
Too old for a snail to dislodge
And someday when I have the time
I will go after you with the razor blade
And clean the sides to see my fish again
But the water is dirty
And I am afraid to stick
My hand in there a second time

Fairy Lights

Fairy lights at the edge of the room
I know we'll need to go home soon
But it's been such a lovely evening

This is what life used to be like
A magic revisited every night
Before we grew up and the world
Went dark and light, pitch black or too bright
With nothing in between

I need you to know I loved you
In my own imperfect way
Brief twinkles in the twilight
Nothing bright or brave

And I understand I'm just one of many
Childish things you've put away
But tonight beneath the fairy lights
We can pretend for a time that nothing's changed

Secrets and Lies

Tell me your secrets
And I'll tell you my lies
Stay with me here
Until I learn how to hide
You're drowning in memories
I don't want to find
A face at the window
And a body inside
Needles and poisons
And laughter at death
And somehow your smile
Is all I have left
So wait in the corner
It's not time to start
But when Fate blows the whistle
I'll play my part

I built my own tower

With coarse red bricks
And no door
I built it
From the inside
I built it
Alone

And installed one small window
In the highest part,
An escape route just in case,
One small source of air and light

The stair inside is winding,
The floors a splinter-full hardwood
Unvarnished,
The walls with no insulation

In winter I am so cold
And I lie beneath threadbare blankets,
My hair bundled tight on my head

You will not weigh it down.

If you care enough to climb for me,
Bring a ladder.

Soul

My collarbone juts out
Like an iceberg, like a shipwreck
Rising from the ocean when the water is low
And with shoulders hunched
I could hold an inch of liquid there
And sometimes I drive my fingers in between
The place where my chest meets my neck
Before I remember—

I am more than a blanket
Of ever-fading flesh
Wrapped tight around decorations
For Halloween
And I have touched something deep
Inside myself
Which belongs to me, and no one else
And inside my body
Dwells a sacred thing

Live

I want to live but my heart is dry
Like the sea at its parting
Like a body cremated
Like a bloodless wound

I want to live but my soul is empty
Like the sky before a new moon

I want to live but I am dead
No hope in my heart
No thought in my head

These are the days I envy Pinocchio
That boy that was not a boy,
That life unexpectedly lived

I want to be alive but I am dead

Amor Gratia Artis

I have loved you like a piece of art
That is to say
I chipped at your chiseled chest
Every day, but never made you
Good enough to make me
Let you stay.
I loved you late at night
With angry music blasting
And red paint splattered
Furious at your frame.

Art is like a phoenix
Which I must kill and burn
So something new may come to life
But you are skin and bone,
Heart and soul,
And it seems that you
Will not rise again.

I Wanted to Tell You

The last time you saw me you grabbed my hand
And wanted to say something but you didn't.
The last time I saw you I waved at the back of your head
And wanted to call you back but I didn't.
So here you are in my head forever
Your stupid black hat flecked with snowflakes
Walking like a shadow away from me,
And we never said goodbye.

The last time you kissed me with breath like ice
And I breathed it in and wanted to tell you
So many stupid things I never told you
And the last time I loved you
Or remembered it
Five minutes ago I wanted to tell you
But your number has left my phone.

The first time I loved you we were on the couch
Watching some stupid show I couldn't follow
And you turned and smiled and it hit me
Immense and painful and perfect
And I wanted to tell you but how stupid would that be
When you were trying to watch some TV fight scene?

The first time you kissed me I froze
Caught for three minutes in everything I wanted to say
And you stared at me so scared until I laughed,
Pulled off a joke about your lips and Medusa's eyes
And never told you how it petrifies me every time,
And sixteen seconds later, the first time I kissed you,
I tried to tell it all without words.

The first time I saw you is hazy,
A memory borrowed from dozens of stories,
From your parents and mine,
The kind of start that can never end in goodbye,
But your shirt was red and your hair was too long
And I just wanted to tell you
I still remember that.

Recovery

You wake up one morning and realize it's over
Everything that made you who you were is gone
And what did you expect, defining yourself
Always by distress and disease?
By people you've loved who never felt the same
By the crippling fear that you'll be left behind again

Now the loneliness is lifted
And it should be better
It shouldn't be bitter
But you have long since made yourself a shell
For an echoing sense of emptiness
And something unfamiliar is filling you

No one ever asks if the shell
Whose snail has shriveled and died
Wants to have a hermit crab inside

All you've known is loneliness
And you don't know who you are in a crowd
It's supposed to be better; it shouldn't be bitter
But you don't know who to be now
You don't know who you are

Genie

Rub a lamp for me
I don't touch dirty things

You took your magic and went away
But I wish I had told you
How I wished I could let you stay

All my lamps are lit with light bulbs
And oil is for cooking
But you made me wish to believe
In something stronger
Than this cement block world
And you made me see color
Where I know there are only shades of grey.

In your absence I remove lampshades
To touch the light and sift through living
Wires to find the spells inside
And I wish I had wished harder
That you would stay.

Dust

Monstrous
It towers above me
That deafening roar
The last sound I will ever hear.

The so-strong pull
Of our final doom
Destruction
Devastation
Demolition
A dusty demise.
My friends already taken
Devoured
Gone.
And I don't want to go.

Plowing ever ahead,
Rushing through
The enemy screams
A war cry,
The inescapable suction of Goodbye.
We cower in its wake.
And I don't want to go.

In silent agony
We pour out our unseen blood
As it touches us,
As it sucks us up.

For repair I am ruined,
Dust to dust I die.
A sacrifice for society:
Destroying me to make things clean.
The buzz, the hum means death.
But I don't want to go.

Monstrous
Ungodly red it looms
My terrible fate

The vacuum.

Break

It's been a long time
So many rehearsals

I've learned how to break
At only the right times
To follow the fault lines
You set for me in the early days
I only fall apart in the right ways

Now aren't you proud?

Now aren't you relieved
At least I control it?
Now aren't you pleased
With the artfully shattered
Pieces of me?

Sure I've forgotten how to breathe
Sure I've forgotten how to be
Anything resembling me
But it's just what you wanted
So love aren't you pleased

With these ravaged remains
Of what used to be me?

Fire

It's all a blur now.

Turn inward—I remember
That much
And find blood and guts
Muscle and bone
And somehow emptiness

And shall I stab out my eyes
For the love I shouldn't have
And never knew?

Smoke tendrils curl round
We should put the fire out

Absolom's father loved him
Still
And we could go like this forever
But my hand has burned to ash

When the monster is a man again
It doesn't matter
Who was hurt
Before the spell was broke

We should put the fire out.

In this labyrinth of memories
I'm losing sight of you
And what you meant to me

But I still remember
This much
That it never goes the way we plan
And foolish children
End their lives for love
And somewhere in Carthage
A lonely woman
Builds her own funeral pyre

So should we put the fire out?

I used to dream
I was a damsel in distress

And wait for you to rescue me
But the dragon has burned you
Past recognition
And past love

I don't know how to put that fire out.

The first murderer must have loved
His victim
His brother
Once
And I wonder
If a Hell was built from his great guilt
Where he begged that the fire not go out

And did Satan really love the Lord?

Pillows smother
Maybe-faithless lovers
And the prince fell in love
With a woman asleep

I wonder when she woke
If she felt this fire we feed

I have lost sight of you
And approach cremation
Where I still look for the dust you are
And where I find that horrid truth

I don't want to put our fire out.

Hair

I was born with mud red brick red
Copper hair
Dark and warm like blood half dried
Which grew out almost white
Half and half for months like a dated dye job
And I am now the kind of blonde
That is delicate, not dumb, the gold that reels
From enchanted spinning wheels, the virgin
Pure that draws in unicorns,
Something sacred and nothing like me
And I want back the soft red mud
Which made no one expect anything

Flower Child

I dyed my hair pink
To be innocent
Invisible
The black pollen center
Of a flower blooming bright and alive.
Until it droops and the petals drop
To blonde I can hide.
Pluck me and smell me
Put me in water
In a vase as your centerpiece
Give me a reason to forget
What lies beneath my blossom
Keeps worlds alive.

Kitten Sleeping

The way my cat pushes soft ears back
Just a hair, just a twitch
And his eyes become only slits—
That
That is what I want to feel when you touch me
Gentle hands and soft, loving my mismatched nose
Memorizing freckles on my paws.
It isn't much—it's hardly even love.
Just give me the comfort to sprawl out and sleep
With paws on top of your hand
Let me breathe deep
And close my eyes
When I know that you're there

Forget Me Soon

Wait till we're alone now
Till we're the only ones in the room
Hold my hand now
We'll look up at the big full moon
Lie and say you'll see me soon
And I'll smile and lie back to you
Kiss me in the moonlight
Lie and say it's all right
We can pretend just for tonight
I don't want to lose you
But some things you just have to do
So don't let's say goodnight
Let's save up all our time
Let's have just one more night
And tomorrow in the daylight
Tomorrow when we say goodbye
Please remember to forget me soon

Lie and say you'll love me till the end of time
And I'll lie and say the same to you
But Love when all the lying's through
Please remember to forget me soon

Garden

You are a handful of seeds
Spilt out on the dirt.
I want a lovely yard
But do not know how to garden
And the last boy sprung up
Like weeds all around me
Choking the life
From all my other plants
And you may grow up a dandelion
Or a beanstalk
Something with thorns
Or yellow petals
But I will water you
Every day
In case you turn into something
That knows how to love
The way I don't

Too Young

Slam my locker
Grab my lunch
Run through hallways
Don't look back
Don't look back

Lunchroom smells
Like a nursing home
We're really not this old

Years fly by
Souls fade to dust
Hearts coated with rust

Twelfth grade
Dying of old age
Life gone by
There's nothing left
There's nothing left

Big sign says
I need a pass
Run through empty handed
No second glance

I didn't know
I was invisible
I'll fade to black
Just give me a chance
Just give me a chance

The bell rings
We sprawl on the floor
Please Mom let's go home

Just a minute more
Can't hear above
The silent roar
With heartache we crumble
Dust blows away

We are too young
We are too young
To be so old today

Sunglasses

It's like wearing sunglasses
You can see everything just fine
But at the edges of your vision
Everything is just so bright
And you turn and the brightness moves
Forever out of reach

Can't take them off cause they're prescription
And a world too dark
Still beats blurred vision
But it's so damn hard
The beautiful things
Just one eternal turn away

Fragile Things

You slipped through my fingers
And broke them off
A handful of pearls in a glass blown hand
And we are not the sorts of people
Who fall in love
But life alone is not enough
And I don't know how to be
Empty handed.
Now they throw rocks at me
Whose every part is transparent
Decorative plaster stones, but painful still
And you, I believe, have become a necklace.

Dear Somebody,

Don't touch my neck
Don't touch my hips
Someday soon we'll discuss the lips
Keep your shirt on, keep your pants
Please don't expect some grand romance
Please remember I'll do
The best I can

Sometimes I ramble, sometimes I rant
I'll always make you keep your pants
Please talk, I'll listen
Please play with my hair
Please don't mind if I sometimes stare
Take me to movies and make me dance
I'll try if you help me take a chance

Dear Somebody, we haven't met
Dear Somebody, don't hope much yet
We'll have to see what I can give
We'll have to see what you can get

Love
    Me

Songs for Snails

Do you remember
How it was when we were small?

We used to play music for the snails
Collected, careful, from beneath the rocks
In our childhood backyards

We filled glass jars with soft black dirt
And begged our dads to drive nails through the lids
For air holes

And when night fell we took our new friends inside
Dumped them out of jars onto black construction paper
On our mothers' kitchen tables
And took turns on the piano

We picked out simple tunes, dirty fingers on ivory keys
And watched the snails dance
Trailing slime in pretty patterns

Do you remember
When we watched the snails dance?
When things were simple
Our whole lives contained
In three adjoining yards?
Do you remember the days
Of dirty hands and fumbled tunes
Of endless sunny afternoons
Nestled in soft black dirt?

Griseld

There are worse things in the world
Than you—tar and feathers, lynching,
Werewolves perhaps
But I have been touched
By none of these things
And you are a vampire that feeds
On everything I have and I thought
I could bring you into the light
And make you a real person again
But I was wrong.
I have been patient
As you drank away my plans
My friends, my freedom, my trust
And I have been patient
As you trampled all the flowers in my garden
And crumpled up my dreams
As you stripped the clothes from my back
And the shoes from my feet
But there is no more blood for you to take
And I will not be made a monster like you
So here is where my patience ends.

When I've Loved You

When we sit on the hood of my father's car
Eating popsicles and counting stars.
When you call time out to check on me
Because that foam bullet to my thigh
Could have hurt so much,
And when you tell me everything I never wanted
To hear about your favorite video game
And you try to protect me from bad words
On the internet and I want to strangle you
And kiss you at the same time.
The look on your face
When you realize that I'm laughing at you,
When you remember again after six months apart
That I am a grown up too, just quietly.
And the six hours we spent watching Japanese prank shows
On Youtube in my bedroom before our parents missed us,
And the shapes we find not in the clouds but in the gaps between trees,
And when you heard me sniffing upstairs with allergies and you got
So worried that I was crying,
And the long afternoon we spent in the back of your van listening
To your family argue and the secrets you told me in the backyard,
And the moment I realized no one else in the world
would ever take your side.

And I wonder if you know
When we see each other I keep a tally of your hugs in my head
And the number is never high enough and next month my cousin is graduating
And I will drive one hundred miles to see that ceremony
Only because it happens the same weekend as yours.
And I am old enough now to know better
Than feeling like I do when I look at you,
So when I come to your graduation I will pretend
I am here for her but I wonder if you will ever know
I've only made this drive for you.

32

Difficult

I find you difficult to love
But persevere

I remember the long aching hours
That stretched into endless months
When I, myself, was unlovable
When I was a wild, untamed thing
Shaking with energy not my own
When I was a black hole
Devouring whole houses of joy
When every shadow held
whatever I most feared
And I slept with every light on
When at every task I became Sisyphus
When I treated every bite of food like poison
And shrunk into a skeleton

I remember
You stayed
You always stayed

I find it difficult
But stay
As you did

Cherry Trees

Take me home to the cherry tree woods
Take me home to the land where love grows
Take me to where the air is still damp and thick
And everything feels real.

Take me to that small white split level
With the walls all faded and full of splinters
With the back yard full of hard packed dirt
And sad brown prickles we pretend are grass.
Find me the tree where we carved our names
When we were still too young to know clichés

Eat apples with me on the sagging back step
And tell me this will always be real
Wander through forests holding my hand
Show me so I can believe
Take me home to the cherry trees

Song of Self and Shadows

I sing a song for severed souls,
And you, if you like, may listen.

I read and disband my Self,
I read and I watch and I join the sky.

I live to see the lilacs bloom,
And when they die I'll live for roses,
And peonies full blown, petals dissolving in my hands,
And I sigh and sing in silence,
And see snow, white,
And seven sought-for souls,
And worms in dirt,
And maids in towers,
And become the air around them.

I celebrate a different song, which is not mine to sing
here,
And I see life from the shadows, and I live the lives of
others,
And catch my own in glimpses and glimmers,
Reflections which bounce from a stranger's mirror.

My hair, my eyes, behind glasses and lashes, are bits of
me that make of me all the secrets I can
sing to you,
Since I know and know you know no others,
Waiting in peace to end the beginning,
Waiting impatient to begin the end,
Waiting unseeing for colors to fly,
Waiting unhearing for silence to fall
Away.

I listen, and read, and watch the world,
I listen, and read, and dissolve in the world,
And I lose my Self,
And I find the souls that are not mine, and I find the love
that is not for me.

Jingling she runs, with bells in her hair,
And I find her, and love her,
And know not who I am,
And splashing, he jumps, so I sing to the sea,

And melt myself down, to cling, nothing now, with
innocence,
And become the dampness in his hair.

I see them in the darkness here,
A child with shoes a size too big, and the way he smiles
at the way the mother ties them,
A girl in a gown, hair bundled for prom, or homecoming
perhaps, for I have begun to forget the
seasons,
A man waiting for something, worth waiting for, for the
way he fidgets and watches his watch,
A world of waiting for what I want not to want, and
wonderfully, want, regardless.

And I sing of myself in a song not mine,
And I see the silence that should be heard,
And become the tree where we all will hide,
The stream in which we will not drown,
The shadow in which you may sink with me,
And I seek a soul to see my Self, and claim it, and lay me
down undissolved.

Coming Home

The river twists beneath my feet
A satin ribbon edged in lace
And I'm almost there now, almost there

It's just beyond this hill here, a little cottage,
Stone and thatch, chimney silent
In the warm spring air

The door's unlatched; it always is
You're not here yet
But I know you're on your way
Following the river from the other side

I'll get started, while I wait
I find the bowls, and mix the dough
And the scent of vanilla fills the house
And it smells like coming home

Mother, Child

A poem for Eve, a poem for Eve
You ate the fruit, you made us leave
But I have had years to learn sympathy.

Mother, child, don't be afraid
The world is big
But growing here has made us brave

Mother, child, you sinned first
But I sinned worse
Now I will keep you safe

Mother, child, grow up careful
Grow up wise
One day, again, they'll be on our side

Peter

I think you taught me to fly
I remember it
Like I remember learning to walk
And to talk and read,
Blurry and far away

I think you wore jeans
One size too big
And I think they were muddy
And ripped at the knees
And I know I chased frogs with you
But they always slipped away
Without their kisses.
You were better than a prince
Back then when things were clear

And you taught me to climb trees
And at night we hunted lightning bugs
Like fairies,
And sat down in wet grass
And counted the stars

And you always shared your lunch.
You were in perpetual need
Of a haircut and your baby teeth
Fell out so much later than mine
And I teased you

And we were so young but now
You're becoming something ancient
And mysterious, that I can't remember,
And I wonder what else I loved before
I forgot
And I wish I still knew how to fly

Memory

You
Are everything to me
And I'm just a careless memory
You revisit on lonely nights

I have loved you with everything I have
And all I've ever asked of you
Is to take me as I am

And all you've ever wanted
Is the girl I used to be
So you come by to chat about shared memories

I want you to know I still love you
With everything I have
And I know you'll never take me as I am

I finally fell into myself
A fully formed person for the first time
With a handful of pills that make my brain work right

And that's when you fell out of love with me
Turns out you're attracted to agony
And the scattered shards
Of who I once had the potential to be

Now you stop by to poke and prod
Try to pull apart the person I've become
And I let you because it's the closest I'll ever get again
To the feeling of your love

Guinevere

Jenny, oh Jenny
I wish we didn't share a name

Guinevere, I am not the type
To forgive
But you are not the type
To be guilty or afraid

You have loved long and deep
And wrongly, Jenny,
But not all sins are yours
Or mine
That bear our name

It is no great gift
To be a queen
And others, too
Must share this blame
Jenny, you
Can have my name

Fallen

We live in the armpit of the Lord
We are those who find the filth
In even the purest things
Or put it there
We are marble heads
On an artist's shelf
Never complete and never quite real,
And we are nothingness
Too small to be the pebble
You caught in your shoe
But someday we will rise
And be worthy of the love
We receive regardless

Counting Caterpillars

I remember the years long past
Long days spent in solitude, days spent in hope
A heart full of dreams that would never come true

The summers I carried snakes in my pockets
And overturned rocks to befriend the worms
The winters I built snowmen and cried when they melted
Springs spent counting caterpillars, falls spent finding moths
Searching for any company to keep
Until I was old enough to see
Even bugs would never love me

I always knew I would always be alone
I used to think I'd get used to it
Used to think someday it would be easy

I've stopped counting caterpillars
Stopped overturning the rocks
But I still check on worms each time it rains
Collect them from gutters before they dry out
Maybe they don't want me
Maybe nobody wants me
But I won't leave them to suffer alone

My Brother Cries

In a dream my brother cries alone; there is no love at
night.
He is the only brother
Who ever heard my cries.
Now trapped in a dream,
I send him my love,
But we are both alone.

Waiting in the dark alone,
Trapped by the night,
I say I feel no love
For a long gone brother
Who never saw my dream,
But I am betrayed by my own cries.

I used to hear his cries,
When he thought he was alone
And lost in his dead dream.
I watched over him all night,
Trying to save a brother
Who knew no love.

But if he'd let me I'd love
To silence the cries
Of a long beloved brother
Who should never be alone,
Trapped late at night
Inside a terrible dream.

In my favorite dream
Of siblings' love,
At the end of last night
I heard his broken cries
As he struggled alone,
And I comforted my brother.

There is nothing like a brother
To save you when you dream,
But in nightmares I am alone.
I cannot find his love
As I cry and he cries
Both late into the night.

At night my brother cries; I dream of love alone.

Temple

People like to tell me
Lately
How my body is a temple
The sacred home of God beneath my skin
The place where hopes and prayers live

But I learned to worship
In a storefront church
In storage buildings and factories
City gyms and the barest bones
Of a building half built
I was raised on secondhand sanctity
Beauty in the broken places
And my body is small and weak and wrong
But I have carved out a space for God to hide
As long as we're here
I don't know how to care how it is inside
And this space is only His and mine

Fishbowl

I carved out my weary, overworked heart
Last year
And put in its place a fishbowl

I scooped out my useless brains
And put in their place
A fishbowl, too

I've made of myself an aquarium
Something clean and clear and empty
Where happy, colored things can swim

It's lovely now
But I've never taken good care of myself
And I know how neglected fish tanks go

Soon enough I'll be a mess
Of scum and slime again
Ugly smelling, dying things
Like the ones I've just pulled out

Here We Are

I never meant to let it go
This way but here we are
At this crossroad where everybody
One day comes, and somehow
I thought I'd reach it
Alone, but here we are.
I have kept my dance shoes on
Though we walk on holy ground
And here we are holding hands
I did not expect the storm
To come so calm
Though you warned me again
And again; now lightning
Dribbles down from a few small
Cracks in the clouds
And you are bleeding
From the forehead
So here we are
On the road I chose
But somehow
I have left you alone

You

When the end
Comes
I hope
It will be you.

When I find
Him
I hope
He will be you.

But there is a branch
The perfect size to sit on
In a sycamore tree
In a yard you've never seen,
And there is a bottle
With a message from him
For me
In an ice-cold stream
You never swam in.

There is a box
On the highest shelf
Where I hold my most secret self
In ancient letters
You will never read.
And there is a tombstone
In a cemetery
That on some days
I still need to see.

And I've lived in hearts
You never knew.

I hope
When the end comes
It will be you,
But there are a thousand
Red secrets
You never knew,
A thousand blue memories
That aren't of you.

It can't be him now
So still
I hope
It will be you.

Hope

I don't think hope is a thing with feathers
I think it's a thing with fur

A twitching tail and bright green eyes
And white, white whiskers a handsbreadth long

Hope is a soft warm weight at your feet
A purring in your ear, in the too quiet times
A rumbling on your chest, through the bad days

Hope is ears twitching against your cheek
As you press little kisses to a velvet soft forehead
Hope is a kitten who loves me back

Bones

Two hundred and six bones
In the human body
And I can find every one
Beneath the torn plastic wrap
That was once my skin

The balls that make my wrist
Turn, pulled out careful
One by one
Are always good for a game
Of marbles
And my skull more than once
Has been a bowling ball
There is nothing to me anyway
So feel free to play
But when you are done
And wrapping me up
I would appreciate
Some duct tape

Not Me

We all live in one studio
Which has never passed a safety inspection
And all we are is cast in plaster
But you will never mold me right—
Not me
You can never pour enough molten bronze
To make me less—
Or more—
Than what I want to be
Not me
So gather up your art supplies
Just go ahead and try.

Daydream

I used to break myself apart in daydreams
Like eating the limbs of a gingerbread man first
Like stripping the bark off a twig
Break myself down to my most essential self
Don't need the senses
Don't need the legs
Don't need the voice
In dreams I never kept my voice
Like the little mermaid, but there's nothing
I want in exchange
(I just don't want to be)

I always knew I was broken inside
I used to fantasize
That it was something obvious instead
Something real, concrete
Something the world couldn't help but see

I always dreamt of broken things
The broken things were always me

Love Poem

Your hair
is a disaster zone
your jeans sit too low
and you have the weirdest sense
of humour

you think
it's funny when
I'm earnest
and all your shows are stupid

you have
horrible acne
and no common sense
and when you play with my hair
it feels good

you tower
above me, shirtless
which makes me uncomfortable
which makes you call me weird
which is true

I fit
beside you
perfectly when we
sit on your couch to watch
stupid movies

and you have
terrible taste in music
and I hate the messiness
of your room when I come
to visit you

and I hate
the way you make me laugh
at stupid stuff
and sing along to
your music

and you aren't wonderful
by any stretch
of the imagination
but then neither
am I

Persephone

Seeds spill bloody across my hands
Bone hard kernels of life and death
And choice.
We gods don't need to eat.

One for the way you raged
When I took you from home
The drama, a flaming chariot
In your mother's garden
And did you see the look on her face dear,
Just think how she'll worry
I thought we had a plan

Two for the loss that hit you hard
Once the deed was really done
The way you wept and longed for home
The way you pushed me away
Then begged me to stay
For taking your home,
Being all you had left

Three for the way you forgave me
For giving you what you'd asked for
And brought new life and light and color
To my valleys of death and ash
The flowers bursting from the bones
The roots that stretched
So the flowers could reach your home

Four for the fun we had
Mixing growth and hope
With dust and sand
And your laughter, love,
When I made you feel more alive
When you said you could live like this
Forever with me

Five for your anger
When we heard they were coming
To take you away
For you are a woman grown
And the choice was your own
And our gardens burned and I saw
You had power over life
But also death

Six for the seeds, love,
For the seeds you ate
A mortal meal made
Of all your love and hate
And six, love, six for the way I can say
Persephone chose me

From the Reluctant Damsel to the Unwanted Prince

You think I'm here to be here for you
To hang on to every word you speak
To stare at your face with stars in my eyes
To beg you to stay, to scream and to cry
To be taken to hurt you, to wait to be saved
To beg you not to die

Babe I'm not the type you save
And now—what a shock!—you've changed
You're just an angry little man
With an angry little plan
To make me pay for daring not to want you

But babe I'm not the type to pay
I will wear crushed velvet
And dance on your grave
You're not some big hero—
You're a c-list bad guy
See this story's not yours
This story's all mine

You think I'm here to be here for you
But despite you I'm here to be me.

Shedding

My kitten has begun to shed
Soft black hair across the floor
Coating my hands when I stroke his back
And I have yet to grow the faintest hints of fur
That come when your stomach has stopped filling up
But I wish I too could leave in a trail behind me
All the pieces I no longer want or need

Everything is rooted too deeply
I cannot be set free by static cling

Ring

If ever I got married
I'd want a certain ring
The kind you find at roadside stores
Tourist traps
You find them in state parks
You find them beside taffy shops

I want a ring from a tourist trap
Two hundred dollars, tops
I want a small ring with a silver band
In which is set a colored rock
Sky blue, blood red, moss green—
It's all the same to me

Just something small and not too special
Something just like you and me

Esther

You walk with your head held high
You will not beg, you will not cry
You are, after all, his wife.
You are the voice in his ear late at night
The trophy he shows in the soft morning light
You are the most subtle seasonings
On the food he eats
You are soft silk dresses
And redemption he doesn't know he seeks.
So let men scream "Let my people go"
We work with the tools we have
And you will be careful and gentle and slow
But in the end he will still let them go

Home

None of us, on paper, are orphans
But we have always known
That we are all alone.
Terrycloth mothers are better
Than those who offer only food
But I remember a real live love
Flesh and bone
Who would never leave me
On my own

How I wish I remembered
How to go home

Bunk Beds

So many of my memories begin this way:
With two girls in a top bunk bed
Giggling, hair slipping out of messy braids.
Years pass
The other girl changes; I stay the same

At eight we are the queens of the sky
We place stuffed animals on each branch of the ceiling fan
Then flip it on and watch them fly
A tornado, homemade

At eleven we are generals, the bed our fortress
We sketch out battle plans,
My mother's Beethoven playing,
And direct our troops on the ground

At thirteen I grow up and put the loft away
In college I move to the dorms
And bring it back to save space

At eighteen we read and study together,
Underlining frantically,
Throwing wadded up papers back and forth

At twenty we huddle beneath blankets
Watching Christmas movies and eating instant noodles

At twenty two we share the bed, sleeping in shifts
She works nights, I work days
And an evicted friend is crashing on her bed
We get only the briefest glimpses of each other
And I resort to leaving little notes
Under our shared pillow

At twenty three we go our separate ways
Me to a job in another city
Her to a grad school in another state
I dismantle the bed again
And settle in to my own lonely space

Freeze

Your skin is the shade of blue
Most often seen
In a father's ruffle-chested high school suit
And I have done this to you
You who mean everything,
An Oxford dictionary in my heart.
I have always been ice cold
And thought you could make me warm
But instead you are turning icy with me,
Something dead with a chip-away smile
And in this weather the library
Will not stay open.

It will be a great romance, perhaps.
At least we will freeze together

Go

Tricycle short and
Plastic
Maybe pink
Low to the ground
And all a blur with me
On top and I want to
Go
Go
Go

And wind and yelling
Behind me
Farther and farther
Behind me
And the pedals fly alone
As we go down
Down
Down

And the ground comes close
And still we go
Mom far gone
Me and the bike alone
We go
Then the petals stop
And still we roll
Then a hand
On my shoulders
And we stop.
I want to go
Go
Go

She grabs my hair
To fix it
And I pull
Pull
Pull

I want to go.

Feelings: Unknown

I find you difficult to love
A stubborn teenage trend-aversion
I should have outgrown long ago

Everyone adores you so much
I don't want to be only part of the crowd

Besides, you're disagreeable
Obnoxious
(Adorable)

And I hover always on the brink
Of feeling one way or another
Do I love you?
Do I hate you?

(Hate would be easier, I'm sure)

I find you difficult to love
It's not your fault, of course
But I would find it easier
If I knew what you thought of me

Lights

I didn't want these things for us
Not us
Not you, at least

You are burnt out yellow
Christmas lights
Tangled in a heap
In your father's garage

And I thought it was my job
To make you beautiful again
But darling, I screwed up

And you will never decorate
A Christmas tree for me
Not me
But darling it's not your fault

I have piled you messily
In a cardboard box
And found you a shelf of your own

Some day some other girl
Will untie your knots
And give you new bulbs

Shy

Alone in the hall
People walking by
They say she's just shy
Don't you know how hard I try?
Words in my mind
Won't come out through my mouth
Everybody so kind
You could treat me like them
I wouldn't mind
Try to be like you
But I'm trapped inside
Myself
Don't you know how hard I try?
Fight with myself
So many words I can't say
Alone in the noise
Silence won't go away
And it's killing me
All I want to be
Is one of you
But I can't seem to do
Anything your way

They say she's just shy
Don't you know how I try?
Unspoken words die
Inside my mind
Alone all night I will not cry
But you never asked me why
Don't you know how hard I try?

Broken hearted
Cold and guarded
This is where it started
I'm not even gonna try
This is where I lose my mind
And they all leave me behind
They say she's just shy
Can't you see that I try?

Breathless whispers
As classes start
All I want
Is to be a part
Of that

I've never been a part
Of that

You're in there
You're where it's at
And I'm stuck outside
Long ago I cried
Now all the tears are dried
And I've just died
Inside
You never even tried

This is where I lose my mind
This is where I die
They say she's just shy
But you never even let me try
Running and shouting
Laughing after class
Leave me crushed
Behind the mass
With a crumpled pass
Won't someone ask
What I'm doing tonight?

Never mind, it's all right
I'll just turn out the light
When we were young I used to cry
You never asked why
Now in solitude I die
Don't you know how hard I try?
But you won't help me
Why?
I'm all alone
So many words I can't say
Don't want you to go away
Please can't I stay?
I could live your way
I'll learn to talk someday
Just tell me what to say
Just show me how to try

I'm losing my mind
You don't have to be so kind
Just let me try
Won't you let me try?
They say oh she's just shy
Don't you know how hard I try?

If I Asked You

It's been so long
It's been so long
I don't know what to say
If I invited you
Would you come in?
If I asked you, would you stay?

We used to be a perfect pair
Not a matched set, but compatible things
Saucer and teacup
Hot tap and cold
Honey and milk

Without you I'm a mess of incomplete things
Cold showers
Dry toast
Sugar without tea

Without you I've been half a heart
Best friend charm without a match
If I asked you, would you stay?

Holy Land

Dear God,
  The birds do not eat from my hands here
   I do not ask them to
  The paint is peeled, the wood is splintered
  And a much scratched plaque
  Reminds me of a long dead man
  Whose story I have never known.
  Somehow, here, I have made a home.
  The grass is not soft beneath my feet
  My ears are not filled with the buzzing
  Of bees on this ancient park bench
  On a busy city block
  That is nothing like a park
  And through this smog I could never hope
  To see your face
  But closing my eyes I can hear,
  Even here, your whispers in the dark
  So I have chosen this bench
  As the holiest place

Moving On

I would have waited
If you'd asked
Would have waited months or years
If you'd only promised to someday come back

But you didn't

Now the space I once carved out for you
Has filled back in with other things
And I don't know how to clear them out—
Don't know if I want to

I would have given you anything, everything
But you've ceased to be the center of my world
And I don't know what I have left to offer
Don't know if you deserve it

I would have waited
If I'd known there was something to wait for

But I didn't

Now with nothing promised, I've moved on

Conspiracy

My aunt wishes to infiltrate the Freemasons
And learn their secrets, and I still half believe
That water kitties will creep from a cornfield
To drag me away.
The full moon
Makes my mother's students grow wild,
Though they have yet to grow fur
And snouts and tails,
And I think some days that you
Are a patchwork of my childhood dreams.

This is why you have yet to meet my father.
I have hoped hard enough, before, to create
Reality
And faced with facts I have always seen only
The story.
So here is one more superstition:
If I share you, you will dissolve away
Another secret to someday grow up
And disbelieve.
Our love is my favorite conspiracy theory.

Marin

She is a bag of blood and bones
In raspberry lip gloss
And leopard print sneakers
Trying to be a real girl.
Iron aberration on a steel tube,
Plaster handprint on a mother's stone heart,
A crystal bird in flight,
Her secrets hide
In the marbled carpet
Of the apartment where she doesn't spend
The nights

Past

Nothing but sunshine
In the rearview mirror
More fitting than the rainy cliche
All the past is golden
And now I'm moving on
All the past is perfect
Now all the past is gone

Everything behind me is rosy
The ancient tree house
In a neighbor's tree
The circle of grass
At the end of the street
Tangled ivy growing past lilacs
Worn stone steps
With strange bugs beneath

Every tea party we used to have
Apple juice in tiny cups,
Sugar cubes eaten plain

Adventures in unfinished basements
Bike rides to get ice cream
Books we read together
Though we read at different speeds
Books it hurts to read, just me

And all of it disappears
Shrinking behind me on a sunny day
All the past is golden;
Now all the past is gone

Bathsheba

You are my King.
So why should I care
What you do to me?
Take my husband
Take my life
Make me your one thousandth wife
Give me a child
I didn't want
Then take it away with your sin
Just when I've given my love again

I will be your whore,
You *godly* man
What does it matter
When my husband and child are dead?
Why should I care
When you are my King?

Remember

I could write
The lie
Of our whole lives
And leave it here
For you to find the truth
In the decades
That lead your dreams
Away from me
And I could paint our love
Or make it a song
And in a half forgetting future
You could learn
To sing along again
And trace the lines
That still hold our lives
And I'll let you rebuild
Our past
Into something
That for some reason
We could have wanted
To last
And when you have
Forgotten
Who I was
Please remember the kind
Of love
We knew we never had

Kiss

I remember your first kiss
Better, I think, than you do
For I knew even then that it meant the end
Of you and me and childish things
We were so young
And you were so eager to get older
While I only wanted to stay the same

I used to tell myself I only minded
Because I wished it was me you had kissed
I used to tell myself a lot a things
Small lies to convince myself
I had a chance of fitting in

I never wanted to kiss you
I just never wanted us
To grow up at all
Never wanted those hormones to hit
Wanted you to stay forever beside me
Young and uninterested in being kissed

Dreams

In the dark I dream of the dreams you dream
lying alone in bed at home, a hint
of holiness in how the moonlight hits your hair.
I see the sanctity of ordinary things
like how we share our secret dreams,
like how you speak your songs to me.
In darkness I can only dream
of everything you've come to mean.
Have I mentioned that I love you?

Look

He bought me diamond earrings
In a velvet box on a snowy street
Like an ad for some jewelry store
Christmas special and it's too soon
For that right? Too soon
Not that I'm complaining
But look at me, and tell me please
What it is he thinks he sees
Because I am here all
Jagged edges, not the fairy woman
Made beautiful by some man's blind love,
Not the patient wife with flaws
Replaced by greater virtues,
Not some fairy story or commercial on TV
So tell me please
What you think he sees
Because I know it can't be me.

Parking Lot

Crying myself to sleep for no reason
Sobbing in grocery store parking lots
I thought I was better
But then I thought a lot of things

I thought I meant much more to you
And I thought that I could see this through
I thought a lot of stupid things, it seems

My shopping list has been crowded out
By lines of anxious scribbles
All the problems I thought I solved
Always coming back in parking lots

And I am so sick of being alone
So sick of feeling homeless even in my own home
So sick of all of this, but I don't know what to do
Don't think it's a problem I can fix

The End

Rose petals fall
I'm still asleep
the apple's bit
and now I sink
into the deep.
I still can't believe
this ends happily
ever after

Pull out his heart
put it on my shelf
everything I've done
I did for someone else.
Live happily
to the end of my days
is that coming soon?
can we end early?

Once on a time
here's where it begins
here's where it ends
the rest is just pretend

Hearts in the cupboard
souls on a shelf
everything I have
I took from someone else

When they touch me I die
I scream and I cry
but somehow I never
say goodbye

Is it over yet?
can we skip to the end?
Anyway the rest
is just pretend

Close dead eyes
I'm still asleep
kill myself
every time we meet

I'm sinking so deep
but I still sing in my sleep
they sink down next to me

Skin so white
live in endless night
not going down
without a fight

Pearl teardrops fall
I've done this all
before
can you find the door?
Blood mixed with jewels
these are the tools
to build my own downfall

Dance on hot coals
as I chase my goals
away.
This isn't my day
no matter what they say

My lips are blood
skin white as snow
doesn't everyone know
the purity's a lie?
All we do is try
until we die
but I never said goodbye.
Prince charming don't cry

Diamonds sparkle
in the light
pull away
let's say good night.
Or isn't that right?

Everything I've done
I did for someone else
this is how we kill ourselves

One thousand years
now all that's left
is hearts on the shelf
one thousand years
they're all bled dry
don't quite remember
how to cry
I can't quite say goodbye
today is when we die
just one last time

Everything I've done
I did for someone else
and everything I have
I stole it from myself
now there's nothing else

I'm still asleep
down deep
I sink
finally this is the end
the rest is just pretend

It's better to laugh than to cry

I began by giggling when I hit my head or my funny
bone.
Now lipstick stains my teeth like blood
And it's all just a joke how you strip away my everything
And all my dreams are crumpled scraps of paper
scattered
Around the trash can because you can't even bother to
throw straight
So I laugh until I cry, a string of liquid crystal sparkling in
the light.

You will clasp it about my neck
And I will blush and smile
And giggle a little and lift my hair to make your job
More simple.

Didn't

I remember the days I dreamed of you
The person I knew you'd grow into
Before you didn't

You live frozen in my memories

We planned so many things
We had so many dreams
Of things to do together
But then we couldn't,
Then we didn't

You were going to meet me here
Right here
But then you didn't
You didn't
You never came
You never—anything

I was making a new way for us
You were always gonna follow soon

You didn't
You didn't

I remember the days I dreamed
Of the person you'd someday be
Now I can only dream
Of who you were,
Or who you could have been

Ocean in Love

I have loved in ever-waning waves,
You, and her, and him,
And sometimes even me
But with the phases of the moon
My feelings often drain away
If you can play in the shallows
And wait for a while
I will try to beg
The tide to rise.

Us

It isn't fair that after everything
This is what we've become
Signatures in each other's yearbooks
Packed away in parents' attics
Half-remembered names
The vague recollection of a smiling face

I tell new friends the story of you and me
And I'm terrified
By how much I've forgot
All the details lost
To distance and time

I thought we'd be us forever
But now you are you
And I am me
And I'm struggling to remember your name
To remember your face
Though I'll never forget
What you once meant to me

The Lie of Loving You

Behind a splintered smile
You never understood
Lives the final secret
You never knew
Such hopeless whispers
You never heard
From a tall young man
You never met
In a hidden anguish
You never saw

Under a branch where
You never sat
At a river where
You never wept
Above a shelf
You never found
I hide this life
You never lived

Whispering
Back and forth
Late at night
With you
I repeat myself
In case that will make
My words more true
But still I tell the lie
Of loving you

Prayer

Here is a list of things I need.
Here one, shorter, of all you've given me.
So thanks for that, I guess.
And here is a list of people to help
Only I can't remember all their names
So help these three
And everyone else—
You're God, you know who I mean.
Then the ritual at the end,
I love you God Amen

The ancients poured libations
Twist your cup, give the earth one drop
And now I blink and say
Lord thank you for this food amen
God's one drop through history
And now from me again

I bled myself for a Eucharist
Until my soul was dry
And I can feel what Adam felt
The moment before you breathed
Or the moment after that bite,
Dust and more dust, still draining himself

I do not know when I stopped depending on you.

I have told the same lies so many times
I do not remember the truth to tell you
I keep hoping to say it enough—
I love you God amen—
That it will become the truth again
But my words are nothing in repetition
And I don't know where to look for you
When I am the one who is lost

So I am waiting here please find me
And fill me up and show me where to search
For truth and how much wine to pour for you
And how to mean what I say when I come to the end
I love you God amen

Ghosts

We used to be beautiful things
United and in love
We used to have plans, we used to belong
Together

But everything keeps on changing

I don't know what we are now
I don't know who you are now
How you left me all alone

There are only our prayers left at the table
Ghosts of meals past

We used to be grand feasts and elegance
And now I'm a bowl of cereal
While you—you're not here at all

And I don't know how to be
Without you

Real

Paint me red
Like those Wonderland roses
Make me something lovely
Remind me how to breathe

I have made myself
A science room skeleton
With smiling lips blood red

Take me apart
Remake me please

I want to be real again

Snapshot of a Barn in Summer

I am blue with those light blue jeans too high on my waist
Straw somewhere inside, straw in my hair, hair in my
mouth
And splinters in my hand, hand in the window and
Behind us brothers, in shadow, incidental
Because then there is him
In green and smiling like he doesn't
Now
And the heat and there above us a sky too blue too hot,
too far away
And so much noise beyond us
And the shadows long and hotter than sun
Here in a barn, here before a window he pulled me
through,
Here beneath the shadows where we smiled.

Too Late

It was easy when we lived our lives in orbit
Never touching, always passing through
It was easy to think
Tomorrow there'll be time
Though somehow there never was
Easy to say nothing
When the saying felt too awkward

I had an endless list of someday things
Things to ask you
Things to tell you
Things to show

I never thought there would be an ending
Though I know that nothing lasts
You were as certain as the stars
And just as distant
And now all the sky is dark and pressing in

So many things—
And it's too late now
It's too late now
Did you even know I loved you?

Never

I used to dream
Of you
Every night
The only thing I never told you
Eyes closed, mouth barely open
Your hair damp on the pillow
After a long day in the lake

I left you there alone
And found you again in my own sleep
Awake and beautiful
A light in your eyes
I never saw in real life

The darkness closes in on us
Heavy, unspoken
Our final lie pressing down
One last fight
Drags you from my dreams

"I never loved you"

That single lie
So small
It shouldn't be able
To devour my everything

But then you always believed
Whatever I told you

Some Days

It is all I can do not to stick a knife, quick,
At the wrinkle where my hand
Meets my wrist
And slide back the skin to see what lives
Beneath, what I am inside,
What horrible secret I've managed to hide.
I can see, some days, the blood pouring out
Warm and red and bright.
At other times I know that all my blood is
Dried or frozen somewhere deep inside
Or perhaps I am nuts and bolts and wires
And nothing that was ever alive
And it would not kill me, then, to die
But there are people who love what they see
Of me, outside, and I am not the type
To let them down
So I will not even try

Quilt

I've built a life from patchwork scraps
Trying to make some sense
Of bits of broken, discarded things
A lonely life of leftovers—
All I have to keep me warm

And I know I'm not unique, I know
We are all a patchwork mess
Of things we've loved and things we've lost
Crazy quilts of grief and guilt and joy

But shared pain doesn't hurt any less
Than any other kind
And I still wish I could be
A finished, coherent thing

Salem

Salem, I am the witch
Who loves the Lord
With eyes like burning coal
Golden hair laced with poison
Bones made of snakes
And a silver streaked soul.
Salem, I have done nothing wrong
Unless you have done the same and more
Salem, Salem, you killed me
But I too am a child of God
And I too will rise
Again no thanks to you
So Salem, Salem, don't cry for me.

Classroom

The blackboard, brown, won't erase
One boy has shaved his head
My pencil is yellow, number two
And on lined paper I write with a pen

Calculus, history
Astronomy, nothing left of me

You in the front are wearing new glasses
And I remember plaid skirts, pleated,
Where all the boards were white.
We all looked the same
But you all knew my name

Please send me home to high school

Yellow bus, my back row half size seat
The front office where I lived
For periods two and three
Upstairs classroom with a balcony
Windows look out on swamp and street
Love me, teach me, help me see
One more good day is all I need

Lost and Found

I've always excelled at losing things
My phone, my keys, your love for me
I know I put it
In a special, secret place
So no other girl could come and steal it away
But I hid it too well, hid it from myself
Which is how I misplace all the most important things

If I wasn't such a mess
Would you have been willing to stay?

I know I always lose the things I love
Maybe I shouldn't have loved you so much
Should have left you an unfulfilled crush
Because I always forget how to keep things
But never the pain when I realize they're lost

Goodbye

I stand in the driveway and wave goodbye
Sometime tonight you will call and tell me
You have reached your new home, safe.
We will talk about books and boys.
You will tell me about your new school

Distracted, we will live our own lives for a while
We will remember and call again, on birthdays
Until one day we won't.
There may be a text at Christmas
Until we are busy with new friends, soon.

Today this is everything.

But someday all you have given me
Will be a handful of memories
To share with my children
When I am so old I have forgotten their names.

Garage Sale

Put your dolls in a box
Ten cents each
You don't need them anymore
You don't want them
(You're a grownup, you don't)
The gifts you never kept
Your promises to use
The favorite books you've outgrown
All the toys and pets you love the best
Pick a price, pick a price
Put a price on the fat you don't have
On the hair you've pulled from your head
It's time to sell your sleeping pills
The blood you've let live in your veins
The fear that drives you more than mad
Pick a price, sell everything you have
Good and bad
It's time to start again

Maybe Love

People used to tell me
Nothing lasts forever
And I could never understand—
Some things were for always
Things like you and me

But the last time we hung out
I made excuses to leave early
And the last time you texted
I left you on read
So I guess it's true what they say
Guess maybe love, it doesn't stay

It's so weird I'm still so crazy
About a version of you
I must have made up in my head
I miss you so bad
And at the same damn time
I don't really care at all

Maybe feelings don't ever really change
Maybe I spent twenty five years
Just getting to know you
Pulling off masks one by one
Until I reached a layer I couldn't love

Maybe I loved a man I invented
Maybe I loved one
You shed off like an outgrown skin
Left on the floor, empty and dead

I guess it doesn't matter
Guess either way you're gone
There was never any always
About you and me and love

I Did

Sugared white roses
On a wedding cake
But six years ago
You asked me
To save all the dates for you
In pink tulle and heels and ringless fingers
I tiptoe through the Wedding March
Thinking I didn't think this through
I didn't expect to walk this alone
But there were just too few groomsmen
For one last bridesmaid, me.

Not that you asked, but I do,
Or thought I did.

Salt

Lot, I am sorry
I could not look away
I did not know how not to want to stay
And Sodom may have been wrong
But it was my home
Before you ever were
And I am not good at letting go.
Inside me there are wicked things
But mine are not the first
And mine are not the worst
Of all the sins you've seen
Now I am salt on the harsh sea breeze
My sins may seem small, but Lord,
Forgive me please

Troy, Again

Helen is here
I have seen her in the streets
Which Paris brought her I know not—
There are often golden apples here
Careless strewn about the streets
But in her face I have seen our doom
Troy to fall again
Ilium, land of bloodshed in the streets

And will we welcome that wooden horse
A second time?
Or perhaps a different modern thing
Pulled joyful through the streets.

Humanity will never outgrow stupidity,
Nor pride and cruelty in this age,
And I wanted never to be Cassandra
Cursed, ignored
But I have seen Helen weeping in the streets.

Sometimes I See

At night sometimes I see you
Hiding in my head
The cracks and corners
Between cliffs and storms
Nightmares of labyrinths
And unseeing eyes
You flit here and there
Glimpses behind
Ballgowns and daydreams
At night there you are

Bang

We are all made of glass
Sugar and spice
Silk and lace
Any strength is such a disgrace
But someday you will be surprised
By all the things we hold inside
Because baby I'm a weapon
A fucking hurricane
You didn't think there was a reason
They gave all the storms our names?

Flu

I remember recovering from the flu
Setting a hand on my long-empty stomach
And finding it smooth and perfectly flat
Perhaps a bit concave
Nine years old
And I spent the rest of my life
Consumed by a devastating fear
That my shape might someday change

It did, of course
Shapes do
Puberty, and such

And I have spent a lifetime trying
To squeeze a grown up soul
Inside a little girl body
And only sometimes succeeding

And the only thing worse than losing
When it comes to being small
The only thing worse than losing
Are those long aching days when you win
All you are squished down
Deep inside a shell half the size it should be

Odyssey

Here is where we end.
Here at the whirlpool of us and everything
I choose the monster with six heads.
I will claw out the Cyclops eye and hide
No one will weep for me, no one will weave

I will taste the lotus
I will hear the sirens sing
I will forget the way we were Charybdis,
The way you pulled me in

Here is where we end,
Here where I create my own new odyssey
And you may be Penelope—
I will not be the one who waits.

Understand

We lie on your parents' bed
So innocent
And talk about the stars
And ancient wars
And we are children
And it's fine
Understand I'm not grown up
Not asking you to be mine
Our knees are touching on the couch
While we watch your favorite show
Understand I don't want you closer
Understand I don't want you to go
Just here is fine

Side by Side

We grew up side by side, you see
Never apart until the start
Of adulthood, that lonely time

We come together again
When we can
Scattered moments in the midst of Life

Each time we meet I know you less
You're still growing
Into the person you mean to be

And me, I haven't changed
I haven't changed

And it's true you never promised me
To stay forever the same
But I thought we were a story we'd always tell
And now it turns out
I only last until chapter twelve
And the book of your life goes on without me

Turns out I'm only a plot device
Someone who shared your space
At the start of the journey
Not the one who takes each step with you
Forever side by side

I thought we'd be forever side by side

Some days I think this still might work

My hope is nearly lost to him.
In dreams you still come back,
Though I've begged you not to,
Checking my heart for something forbidden.
He'll be angry, you know—
Even fathers can't always forgive.
Loving you is not allowed.

Paris

I will pull you apart
Piece by piece—
See how it feels to lose everything.
I was a wife and a mother
Before you laid your hands on me
And I am not some frail, porcelain thing
And I am not a trophy on your mantelpiece
I am poison and fire and rage
Beneath this sculpted marble face
And my daughter grows old alone
Beyond these walls
And men have fought and died for my right
To choose
Not to be chosen by you.

I am the horse within which
All of a thousand ships of anger hide
And I am the fire
That will burn your city down
And I may be crying now
But in these tears it is you who will drown.

Love

Sometimes I wonder what love is
If I've ever felt it
If I even know

And I think for me love is this:
The way I felt
Ten minutes after I was told you were dead
That's the only certainty I've ever known

And I want you to know
I measure my love still by this metric
For every new person I meet:

I think I love him
I want to love him
I'll know for certain when he's dead

Morbid, perhaps
But the only metric I have
So hard to tell how much I've loved
Until I've also lost

Free Will

Here is how the world works:
You are a God, not a puppeteer
And life in some ways
At least, is fair
No strings on them, no strings on me
But bad things happen
When will comes for free
And this ink was not meant
For some rhyming religious verse
So let me say one thing:
Some days I would rather
Be a puppet on strings
When it takes too much strength
To stand on my feet
And I wonder how you could cut free
The people who take, who hurt and take
And me when I don't know how to be
A person anymore
So thanks for the choice
But I wish I could choose
To give all the choices back to you

If You Knew

If you knew
Me
In the time when all
Was still
If you saw
Me
Before I was left
With a paint spattered heart
When the voices in my head
Were quiet
And the mouth that might kiss you
Still had a tongue
If you knew me
Before you knew me
I think you might love me still

Remember

Remember
When things were easy?
   Remember Red Rover?
(Please send someone over)
   Bugs, roly-poly,
Beneath rocks, big and heavy
Fights with guns and water balloons
Nights with flashlights—no moons
And my skin all speckled
   With mosquitoes (which somehow
remind me of love)
   Three hours in the tree house
On a cool night alone
And the hidden things
Behind herds of moving trees
   (where once I had a home)
A corner of the picket fence
Blocked in by ivy
And a twisting, dying, climbing tree
My legs half made of mud
From long exposure to the creek
   (Here at home I know who to be)

Simulacrum

I am the girl
You fall in and out of love with
Before you know my name,
A half formed dream
In your seat on the train
You rush to say hello
And forget to say goodbye
A golden goblet you didn't see
Was made of cardboard inside
My smile shines.
Beneath I am oak leaves and poison ivy
Easy to hurt and be hurt by
Emptiness, blue-eyed

Astronomy

I see you like a star
Not beautiful and glowing
In a world too dark
Though you are
But a thousand thousand
Light years away
Impossible to meet
In the present
Face to face

You are all the night sky
And even the finest telescope
Can never keep you close to me

Trapped

Little things keep escaping my heart
Things I used to love—
Now all the feelings are gone
And I don't know how to coax them back

So I'll coat my heart in cling wrap
Hold every lasting feeling inside
Close the doors and put in locks
Now all my loves are trapped

Game Night

I used to find it boring
Always the same
Roll your die, skip three squares
But now I am angry
Now I am afraid
Because the rules always change
And I am always a pawn
In someone else's game
And I never even asked to play
The dice never roll my way
And the wrong cards always come up
And someone else is always the judge
I suspect you of cheating at Go Fish
And you never explained the rules of chess
And they say the King has to have a Queen
But I would rather play Old Maid
So this is me declaring war
Get a clue. I'm through with all of you
I won't do game night anymore.

Glasses, Masks

I am wearing bulletproof glasses
But they come at me with axes
There is nowhere to hide
I can only close my eyes
And once, I swear, I was not alone
But I can't remember how to share a home
The world is large
And the world is hard
All I have is this mask
And all they do is hack
And the shattered glass will destroy my eyes
But if you asked nicely I might try
To let you, just you,
Meet the face behind my masks

Enchantment

When you were a songbird
I was your song
When I was a sailor
You were my sea
I ran the numbers and every time
We were a beautiful equation, you and I
Our love the sum of everything

But magic and math, they never last

Now you're just a man
And I'm just a woman
And everything between us
Is just long division

If I could go back I'd beg myself
Not to break the spell
Enchanted you were my everything
And now you're a stranger
I don't want to know

Stop

I just
Want it
To stop.
Just for a moment
Just for a day
Just forever, I want to stop.
I can't solve the rest.
But we all in middle school on the internet
Learned how to make our own time
Go away
So here I dissolve
Myself
Body after mind
And you think you can save me, but my heart
Didn't break that way
And you don't know the patterns to find
And put the puzzle piece chunks of me
Back in line.

Medea

He was four years old
Skin a shade lighter than mine
Midnight dark hair in wispy curls
A wobbling walk
Crinkles all over when he smiled

He was lost in the morning
In the rain

When he was three years old
I remember
Small legs in red shorts
Pumping furiously
On a plastic tricycle up a hill

When he was two years old
We hid behind walls
To eavesdrop on his father
And un-understanding he laughed
And I made him soup from a can

When he was one year old
The first word he knew was my name
No grandfathers gave him gifts
So I sewed all his clothes and toys
And toothless he smiled at me

When I bore him unborn
His father kissed me and sang my praise
And I watched unweeping as my brother died
And thought at least I had good
Somewhere deep inside

Today he would be fifteen
Deep tanned skin and large calloused hands
Shining thick black curls
Above dark eyes
That crinkle in the corner when he smiles
Short like his father and mine
And smart and strong and brave and kind

My stepson across the table
Tall and fair and just fifteen
Laughing
Passes a plate in my direction
And I clutch my butter knife

This one I must not love

Sky

Let us go, love, you and I
To the place where the hillside meets the sky
A sunset horizon, burning bright

Let us sleep, love, you and I
Beneath the willow weeping, along the riverbank

Let us retreat, away from this place
To lands where things are simple
You and I and the open sky
Freedom and beauty and peace

Let us go, love, you and I
To the place where the hillside meets the sky

Cassandra

Listen.
I speak in smoke and curtains
Murder weapon icicles
An unphotographed Bigfoot you barely
Missed
A wooden horse that doesn't rock
A silent jack in the box
Are all I have to my name
I, the woman with words
Beneath my tongue like toads and jewels.
I loved a man once,
Who has kept my oft-kissed lips
And now I cannot make my words direct

Never the Same

Like a nightmare,
Swan's daughter sold
For an apple, like a slave,
But the seller never owned her.
Taken by the sea foam,
Taken by the evening star.
Given to a prince
Who was the flaming torch,
Destroying her whole world.

One hundred ships,
One thousand ships to save her.
One million wouldn't matter.
No escape from the evening star.

Ten years.
Ten years with the prince,
With the flaming torch.
Ten years like a Nightmare,
Then came the Horse.
Freedom like water,
After a long, long drought.

No more prince, no more endless war.

But it isn't the same.
The taking was a nightmare.
The return is waking up
And realizing
You never slept,
Ten years gone by,
And nothing is the same.

Your beauty gone,
And you realize
You don't know
Who you are now.
Ten years is forever,
And then some.
Your life has gone on
Without you.
Home again,
But it isn't the same now.
It's never the same.

Feline Love

We speak of puppy love
But I have always cared like a kitten
Vicious and desperate, needy and mean
My affection is feral and young
And I will always bite the hand
That feeds
And I will hiss and scratch
And rub hard against you
When I am in the proper mood
I will be angry and selfish and cruel.
But never believe
That I do not love you

Danae

A woman in a window
Is watching me
With wide sunbeam eyes
Like light, and hope, and death
And I cannot look away

There is a woman in the water
In a pine box, coffin with no paddles
And a child sobbing
In her lap

A boy stands before me
With his mother's sunbeam eyes
And I could kill him with my ice storm gaze
I could

But this one I will let win
A woman in a window
Is watching me

Never Land

I hate outgrowing the people I love
A new, disgusting, enlightening feeling—
Usually I'm the one left behind

And growing up alone is hard

I wonder how many old friends
Sat waiting all night at my window
While clueless, I played in never land
And returned dismayed to find them gone

I wonder how many old friends tried this hard
I wonder if when they finally left
They wanted this badly to bring me along

I'm sorry, I can't wait any longer

I've been left behind so many times
And I can hardly believe I could do it to you

But I have to, I've outgrown you, I can't wait at this window
Forever for you to catch up
To the person I've become

And I'm sorry and I hate this and I'll love you forever
I just can't stay here anymore

Sleep

I live in a bunk bed prison cell
Bed springs above me
Where a mattress once lived
Before my roommate went away.
In the night the cat will climb and crawl
And the metal rattles beneath his paws
The wooden ladders are unbreakable bars
From which, in the morning, I cannot escape
And behind which, at night,
I don't want to stay

The Days the Ocean Loved Me

I remember when we met
How all-consuming it felt
I was in love with the idea of you
The only kind of love I knew
Things distant and giant and pure
Like the forest, like the ocean, like God

I remember the days that followed
Dizzying, the joy of them
So much so I stumbled
And lost my way

In the end I gave you everything
Everything I never meant to surrender
And some days I can hardly remember why

But the rest I'll never forget
How it felt for one glorious moment
When I knew the ocean loved me back

Siren

Fingers dance like whispers
Across your skin,
The lightest brush of nails
Her eyes are all the colors
Of the ocean
Staring lovingly down at you
She speaks in love songs or lullabies—
Words you don't know
In unmistakable tones,
Gentle enough
To drown out your screams

Fairy Tale

Once upon
A time
In the land of sleeping
Rape victims
Where necrophilia
Reigns supreme
And women are sold
To vicious Beasts
Or locked in towers
To destroy their dreams
I wait for Prince Charming
To show himself
And ravage me
Isn't it just lovely
How we always end so happily?

Twist

We twist ourselves silly
On the merry go round
Beneath a green cloud sky
Backyard carousel, rusted handles, breath held
They say green skies mean twisters
But we're so dizzy on our own
It might be nice to spin up high

We are still young
And danger is nothing
But a different kind of fun
We'll spin any way the wind can ask
As long as it will spin us fast

No

This is how the story goes
We meet in May
We take it slow
In March you move to kiss me
I step away, say no
Yes I want to be with you
No, I have not been hurt before
Shredded from the inside out
By some man with a silver smile
And stainless steel fingernails
My heart is not cold
Nor is it an open sore
But I have never danced
To the songs you expect

My body will remain undriven snow
But I love you with all my tarnished soul

Graduation

I have coughed up the dust
That has lived in my lungs
Leaving my dorm for the final time
To go home for one last summer
And I am too young to be cracks
In the asphalt road,
Raindrops on windshields blocking the view
Too young to be uprooted trees
But here I am, a fistful of splinters
From your backyard swing set,
A mug of hot chocolate
On a humid day
Brand new, already worn thin
Knock-off of a brand name toy
In a department store,
Ready to live a life of my own

Proserpina

I am the Iron Queen
I am Kore, the girl
Proserpina, Persephone
I took hell and made it
Mine

Here are the pomegranate seeds
Shining red blood drops in my mouth, shining red blood
I have tasted death, six drops in my mouth
And it is sweet

I am the Sybil, Scheherazade,
I sing in the gilded cage
The songs to save my life
Half, then half again
But as I shrivel in body
My soul breaks free

I chose this, you see
And I'll choose it every time
I will eat the lotus and begin again
And nothing will change
I will always free myself
I will always reclaim this hell
And you will never hurt me

First

We're sitting on the couch
Just watching a movie
You lean over and kiss me
My first, from you who I met yesterday.
And I, the woman in the Barbie wristwatch
Am expecting something magic
But mostly it feels damp.
You kiss my neck and it tingles a bit
And I wonder
What will happen in the movie next.
When you push me down I don't say no
And am coaxed to remove the leather coat
In which I have hidden my knife

So this is what a first date is like.

Lotus

Here
Are half remembered dreams
Here
Are love and hate for you and me
Here
Where the flowers bloom eternal
As your good humor did not
One detail so clear
In a haze of blurry snapshot memories,
All of you I've bothered to keep
Though I think I would shed this too
If all potions for forgetting were not a lie
I do not think now
Of you in a jersey for a sport you don't play
I do not think now
Of your smile lopsided
Which pulls to the right
I do not think of plans we made when you still spoke to
me
And I have never once wondered
Whether you even remember my name

Showing and Telling

I baked all my love in a blueberry pie
Stitched it into each seam of that quilt
I thought I could say it
Without having to say it
I guess actions don't really
Speak louder than words

How could you not know I loved you
With everything I had
When every note I sang was yours
And every stroke of every brush?

I loved you in every way I could
You never even knew

On a Dragon

There is only dust now
Floating in the wind from passing cars
And the world is full of smog
But glints of silver will haunt
The corners of my eyes forever.
I won.
Her hair is still tangled in my teeth
Singed and slightly bitter
And scraps of white silk are scattered
On the ground.
Well, I didn't start it.
But eating sheep and hoarding gold
Has never made me friends
Is it so wrong, I want
To look pretty?
The jewelry fit me better
And it's all smoke now
Useless paper money in the breeze
And silly people who think
I care
Falling to their knees
And I am so tired
Of all of this
And can summon no more flame.
But I remember when fire
Filled the skies
And most of it was mine
Back then when I was strength
And beauty
Before they came with their tanks
And their toothpick knives
And made me only death.

Me

Been a long few years of ups and downs
Been a while since I knew my face in the mirror
So I slip into old selves
A ghost possessing my own body

My high school uniform still fits
I wear it and try to be that girl again

Found my first pair of glasses
From when I was ten
I can't see a thing and they don't fit my head
But I keep them on so I can pretend

I want so bad to be that kid again

If I could just find a person to be—
(It doesn't have to be me)
If I could just find a person to be

You Brought Me Flowers

Pale pink carnations
Wilted in your dirty hands
Good enough for now.

For Boys I Wasn't Meant to Love

I was the pastor's daughter
Sitting alone in an eight person pew
And you were the stoner
Looking for a place to charge your phone
And you had piercings
And this gorgeous hair
And I wanted to beg you
"Take me away from here"

I was the teacher's pet
Peer reviewing for extra credit
And you were the class cutter
Who didn't know if it was there or their
And you told me jokes
About things I didn't get
And if you'd thought to ask me
I'd have cut class with you

I was the new girl
Trying to work like it was a job I loved
And you were the lifer
Deep frying fries like it mattered at all
And you had this smile
When you reset my grill
And I'd have lived for fast food
If I could've lived there with you

I was the virgin with a purity ring
And you went through girls
While you flirted with me
And I almost believed it meant something
If you'd dated me
I'd have given you everything

I was the good girl
And you were the boy next door
With the motorcycle
With the record
With that bouquet of roses
When you knocked on my door
And you listened when I begged you
"Take me away from here"

And I loved you all
And shouldn't have
And won't apologize
Not for the love
Or for the lies
But please remember me
When I remember to be me
And leave here to be good again

Hearts

I am wearing a crop top
And high waisted leggings
Boots, black with buckles
And my hair is pink
So I wonder what you think of me

I am harsh and jagged
Boiling anger spilled over the edges,
Sharp and shattered,
Of my sober wineglass heart

I am soft and smooth
Giggly, wide-eyed, hopeful still,
Fish swimming clear for all the world
To see in my aquarium heart

Maybe

But we wear the armor we have
And beneath my leather jacket
You will never see
Exactly what I am

Rapunzel Rapunzel

Rapunzel Rapunzel, let down your hair
That braided rope of sunshine and daffodils

Rapunzel Rapunzel, let me up
The lifting may hurt
But the result will be worth
The pain

Rapunzel Rapunzel, I'll break down your walls
From the inside, let you out into the world

Rapunzel Rapunzel, I know you're afraid
But Rapunzel Rapunzel, I'll show you the way

In the Suburb Where We Lived

Paper routes and popsicles
Ice cream cones and apple juice
Playing in snow and playing in sand
Running through sprinklers
With all of you

We climbed that tree
In the backyard
A thousand feet high at least
And I fell and scraped my knee
But you were so strong
And I didn't cry

I lay in the dirt
In my new white dress
You laughed with me so innocent
This I know was what love is

Lies

I have always been good at telling lies
No, I don't mean that
Yes, I'm fine
But today the truth is half chipped away
Like bright red nail polish, one week old
And all I feel is cold inside
I forgot how much I had to hide
Beneath layers of hairspray and lipstick,
Secrets and lies
But the truth could never
Have made you stay
So I'm sorry you found out this way
But the things that have settled deep
Between my bones are only mine

Story

My imagination grows limp with longing
And my fingers ache to create
But I have no story to tell

Or none that I can tell in words

I tried to weave my life
With yarn on a cardboard loom
And I tried to bake myself
Into cookies, chocolate chip

I stitched my story in a purple skirt
I tried to paint it,
To draw it,
To carve

All I got was messy

I could vacuum my history
Straight into the carpet perhaps
But who would read the floor for secrets?

Cressida

Dear Troilus
    I have moved on
    Beyond the dull stone walls
    That once contained our love.
Dear Troilus
    You loved me like
    A picture in a magazine
    But I am a real girl, 3D
Dear Troilus
    We loved like wind and fire
    Like drowned cats
    Wet and angry and mean
Dear Troilus
    We loved the way we were told
    In cartoons in our childhood
    Like all that glittered was gold
Dear Troilus
    Stop writing me
    Across a thousand miles
    I have learned to breathe alone again

Triumph of Icarus

He leaps from the roof, Icarus reborn.
Sees the sliver of red—a flower in the green green trees, a
yellow-clad dreamer, a cut on his arm.
He looks back at the edge of the platform he jumped
from—it is about to fall.
The air smells of palm trees, of courage, of spring.
No feathers for Icarus, no wax to melt. He flies over the
street in jeans and a T shirt.
Speed and momentum, jump carefully planned. He will
not fall.
The sun is bright, it is hot: wings would melt, if he had
them.
The yellow-sweater-dreamer watches, as he loses all
fear.
Below him he sees the Labyrinth of the streets.
Icarus reaches the edge, victorious, leaves the mundane
world behind.

Together

Here we are at opposite ends
Trying to stay together
Coming out all untethered
Again and again and again

I've wanted a lot of lavish things
Not diamonds and ponies
But the kinds of loves
That only, I've learned, exist in stories

Maybe all our friction
Is that we treated each other like fiction
But then that's how I've always
Treated myself
And isn't that the golden rule?

I never asked, you know, to be real
But if I must be I wanted
To be real with you
A pity it didn't work

Happily

They say fairy tales are the games
That only little girls can play
So tell me then please
What is our prize?
Because all girls must be patient
And all girls must be kind
And we must be loving and giving and gentle and wise
And we must be obedient, and never too Curious
And win all our hope with subterfuge
And we must not be weak
But we must not be strong
And I will give you my hands, sir,
If you will spare my foolish father's life
And I will give you my child, sir,
To save myself from his foolish lies
And I will prove myself to princes again
And again
When they can't remember my name
And I will keep silent when they accuse me
Of crimes
And put me to flame
So tell me again, if this is a game
I am destined to play
What, when I win, is my prize?

Teenage Girl's Room

In the very back of the bathroom cupboard
lie unopened bottles—
forgotten gifts
from well meaning people
who never knew you

Nine year old diary
behind the bookshelf—
your handwriting's improved
(spelling's the same)

Twenty Agatha Christie books
you bought at a garage sale
for a nickel each
and an instruction manual for guinea pig owners
but the guinea pigs are long dead
you have a hamster now

Leotards that don't fit anymore
from before you learned you couldn't dance
buried in a box of dress up clothes
you never wear now
and a red wig
you bought in a moment of foolishness
(really, what did you think you'd do with it?)
hidden at the back of your closet

The Barbie collection
you aren't ready to lose
in another box
next to it

The dress you bought for a dance
no one took you to
still hanging up
never worn

Two dozen half empty notebooks
waiting for you to know what to say

The birthday card your brother gave you
and a badly tie dyed too big T shirt

A stuffed dog named Hippo
who doesn't have a nose

A mysterious note on an origami swan
a number you know you'll never call

The minutes from your secret club's last meeting
two or three years ago
a prayer journal you've never used
but you keep it anyway
because it came from a friend
you'll never see again

Pictures everywhere of you and your friends
all from years ago when you still knew how to be a kid
none from recently
because you haven't learned to be a grown up yet
and you don't know what you are now

These are the secrets of a teenage girl's room
the memories that define you
the things that make you
what no one can know
what no one can see
the things that make you human
different and just like everyone else

These are the secrets of a teenage girl's room
the things that no one can ever see

Nicotine

There's something sweet in the smell of tobacco
Something that calls me home
It's the smell of childhood Christmases
Before the grownups got smart and quit
Some little girl part of my heart insists
Cigarettes are for grandmas
And I linger in parking lots looking for love

Perhaps I'll die of secondhand smoke
And perhaps that's just the price
Of hanging on beyond the time
You know you should have let go
But still I hang like dirty smoke in the air
Of the memories I should have left behind

Here

Are shadows and secrets and lies
Are all the things I've tried to hide
Are sins in gold leaf,
Upside down dreams,
The slime that grows in the back
Of my mind,
And all the trampled snow I've left behind,
Fragile white flowers, which are lost loves
And pieces of art,
And all the dead fish
That float in my aquarium heart.
Here is the box,
And here are the locks,
And you will never get inside.

Books

Of three hundred and seven books in my bedroom,
Five were gifts from you.
One is dark blue and heavy, with tattered pages and a
musty smell
Like a flowerbed after spring rain.
Another contains love poems, all ancient and iambic.
One is a cheap paperback I never read
And one was published by your sister.
My favorite is a picture book you bought me in a shop
downtown
On a cloudy cold day in March
When we missed our bus and sat on a dusty floor
Reading children's stories all afternoon.
This morning I packed them in a box
With my Bible and my Spanish dictionary.
Tomorrow I will move out of my parents' house.
Tomorrow I will pretend I have moved on from you.

Glass

I am shattered glass
On the pavement, your finest crystal
Carrying apple juice for a child
And you thought this would end all right?
I am an elegant, delicate thing
Shiny and clear for the world to see
And I deserve so much more
Than you've given me

And I have become cracks in windshields
Chips in your china
Bathroom mirror full of sticky fingers
Signs of real life, insidious and mean
So treat me how you treat me
But know that you made me
What I am,
A glass that always leaks

Mine

We played tic tac toe with sticks and stones
Giggly drunk on mulberry wine
For all those hours in that mossy knoll
That summer I knew you were mine

But the spot that once held my love for you
Is now nothing but a festering wound

At night I dream of the dreams I dreamed
When you still slept beside me
And the birds still sing, but not for me

I no longer sleep outside, for fear of racoons
How they come at night to lick the wounds
Of the parts of me that used to belong to you

(It's kindly meant, but I don't intend
To gain rabies on top of losing you)

It's over but still I go back every night
To that long hot summer when you were mine

My mother is a hoarder but it's fun

My kitten is a jungle cat,
According to my dad
And we explore the basement
Like it's a foreign land
With boxes of beehives
And eagle feathers we aren't allowed to have
A dozen-dozen toys and games
We might someday need when there are kids Again
And I jump and climb through
Cardboard boxes and plastic bins
In search of old photos
And find my grown up brother's
Second grade artwork instead.
If I ever need a single crutch
One is here waiting for me
Along with eleven years worth
Of Christmas gift bags
And together the cat and I will discover
New worlds in a pack rat's home.

Slippers

Fuzzy pink slippers
You gave me
For Christmas
Long dead joke
I am not your Cinderella

You chose the ugly
Stepsister, me
With cement block
Tugboat troll feet

Size twelve prom shoes
Tight red dress
In the back of the room
You said "dance
With me," unlaced
My shoes and kicked them away
Barefoot, not your Cinderella

Seven years, PHD, ugly
Boots as I study
All night saying "please
Don't leave"

I will wear your slippers
If you keep choosing me

Morgan

His love for you is warm and needy
Hardened hands on your sun-baked skin

His love for you is hot and hard
Calloused fingers pulling
At your fragile spider web hair

His love for you is burning violent
Bracelets like shackles on your wrists
Bruises up and down your neck
Purple-black beneath your eyes
Nails gnawed on and lips chapped
He has a careless dragon heart
And the heat will turn you to ash

Morgan, choose me instead

Spring

Oh give me another of those late
Warm springs I remember
From when I did not mind the melting
When the whole earth smells
Of milkweed milk, and a small striped worm
Means hope for better things
And the grass grows green
While the raven sings something
He thinks is beautiful
And maybe his faith can make it true

Oh give me a long gone spring

Remember

"Don't you remember?" he asks
When he tries to carve back out
A place for himself inside you
A place you've spent these last long months
Filling in and sanding smooth
And painting a bright new color

"Don't you remember?" he asks
And you think back
You think back on the hole
He made inside you
You think back and you say

"I remember us
I remember the moment
When you and me
Became you-and-me
When all our plans turned into dreams
When all my projects unraveled
When the unit we were
Devoured the selves we had been

"I remember us
I don't remember you
I barely remember me"

And he leaves

And tomorrow he'll be back
With a jackhammer perhaps

But you've long since learned
To rebuild the walls your love knocked down
And you've gotten good at construction

What he breaks again
You'll remake better

Dead Things

Lotta dead things on the beach today
Starfish, sea urchins, half a bird
A horseshoe crab and all my plans
For the kind of story we would be

I sit among a flock of sandpipers
They've accepted me as their own
Because we're all just picking at bones
And I don't know how to do anything but love you

I already know I'll forgive you
It's what I always do
But for now I watch the tide go out
And imagine it carries away
All the things I've felt for you

Leech

I have always swum alone
But you have latched onto me
You, you leech
And maybe long dead doctors
Were not wrong—
With you on my arm
Even sucking out my warm lifeblood
I feel better

To the First Grader Who Hopped the Fence to Play in My Backyard All Summer

I don't remember your name
But I remember how
When we started school
You were so embarrassed to be seen
With a kindergartener
You paid another girl to chase me away
At recess
In the afternoons you hopped the fence again
And I let you
I played with you
I was five
And I didn't understand

Today I understand
I understand that I have always
Been the stop-gap friend
The stale bread you eat
When the fresh food is gone
The flip phone you use
Until your mom buys something smarter
The thing you leave behind with ease
Pick up again in desperation

I understand exactly what I was worth to you
Which was the swing set in my yard

You are the first friend I remember
And I can no longer count
How many turned out exactly the same

I want you to know I cried over you again last night
You and a thousand other things
You and all the things you mean to me
Which are being always picked last
And being always second best
And being stupid enough to accept
Whatever small gestures I'm given
Every single time

Haiku

In nightmares you come
The beauty of destruction
Rebuilding me here

Motel

My body's not a temple
It's just where I live right now
Not any better than any other
Sad little roadside motel

And every night I put on the lights
Of the neon orange vacancy sign
Because there's no one here now, no one home
I live in myself alone
And I'm so lonely, I'm so lonely

Why take care of a house that's only temporary?
Why vacuum the floor
When you have no friends to visit?
Why keep yourself alive
When you're already dead inside?
Why try? Why try?

My body's not a temple
It's a motel where no one ever checks in
Any I'm so lonely, so lonely
Wandering the empty halls of my own heart
Waiting for something to start
To matter
But nothing ever does

Sawdust

All we have ever been
Is playthings for someone else
Tiny perfect fashion dolls
Porcelain, silk dresses, angel-faced
And fragile
Something soft to hold and love
But I am not good enough, even,
For some asshole's toy box.

I am a sawdust doll
With a hole in the side
All the shit that makes me up
Leaking out into the mud
And the eyes, painted on, are fading

Don't you dare try to save me

Love Story

It doesn't have to be a love story.
Just wander through the silver trees
Just take me to a white sand beach
It doesn't have to mean those things.

We'll lean against the Chaska brick
We'll laugh a lot,
Make something stick.

Please let me wear a pretty dress
This night can end
With a hug not a kiss.

Just stay with me.
It doesn't have to be a love story.

Pretend

I'm not asking you to love me
Just to pretend for a while
Earthworms seem happy in the dirt
But I'm sure some nights they dream of wings
I don't want to be a forever butterfly
Just want to give it a try

Just play pretend with me
Just give me one night of this fantasy
I'm not asking for a real romance
Just a few short hours
To give dreams a chance

Delilah

You are the woman
Who loved money more than him
But he is the fool
Who loved you more than God
Even after a thousand betrayals
And you will not pity him
For this trust so blind.
You won't, you won't
Some things have to be done
Though whispers say they don't
They don't
And love and life are both contests
You've just won
And you don't miss him
You don't, you don't
And you don't need him
You don't, you don't.

Open

I have seen myself in shadows
And someone else's dreams
And I'm not sure how
To be just myself

I am not a Persian rug
On your hardwood floor
Not a credit card to beg you
Take more and more
I have open eyes and an open mind
But once you closed all my doors
And I don't know how to tell you
I'm not that girl anymore

I have changed all the locks
And if I need, again,
To close myself up and hide,
You will be on the other side

Game

It used to be a game we played
Now it's become the life we've made
And I don't want it anymore

It seemed easy then
Hopping back and forth
Every day a new square on the board

But I'm so sick of trying not to lose
When all I wanted
Was to be in love with you

It seemed so easy
Every win a revelation
And I thought I could keep up
But you held all the cards

I only want you, win or lose
Don't want our life to be a fight
I just want to be with you

War Call

Find me the king of the western sea
Find me the queen of the storm
The dust is rising from the east
The drought is coming home
So beat your plowshares into swords
This is the call to war

Bring me rubbish
Bring me gold
The orders are coming
But we'll choose on our own
So don't back down—not here, not now
This is the call to war

Gird your loins
And grab your bows
Make your stand and take your sword
Close your eyes and just hold firm
The troops are roaring through the storm
This the call to war

To Sir Gawain

It is possible
That I am not enough
To cause you anything but pain
And it could be
That you think I am the small devoted dog
That will do as you say
But I am built
From all the best of broken things
And I do not exist to obey your whims
I could be the lady who rejects the knight
Who doesn't deserve to be alive
But I am all the kindness
Of morning fog that clears away
To show the jagged rocks not quite too late
And I am the hope
Of the first small bud of spring
And I have chosen ugliness
Which if you are worthy
Will not chase you away

Parable of the Seeds

Lord make my heart a fresh tilled field
Open up my soul
I want to feel things again
Want the lovely things to last

Lord all I am is rocky ground
Dirt packed down so hard
I can hardly feel at all

Lord the rain, it bounces off my back
Never sinks in at all
And Lord I'm so dry, so tired
So sick of being all alone

Lord I want a heart where the good things grow
Where worms can dig and bunnies burrow
Lord I want my heart to sprout poppies and roses
Tomatoes and beets and sweet, red things

Lord make my heart a fresh tilled field
Lord let me feel alive again

Winter

Grass, green, pokes through the snow
Nothing at all like hope
Spring is half here but I hate the heat
Cling to the numbing cold

My ears hurt so much
They have disappeared entirely
And I cannot see through my glasses, fogged
Everything white
And soft
And safe
And sometimes I can believe
I don't exist at all

Superman

I am not the kind of girl
Who will watch in awe
As you save the world

I am the one who follows behind
To pick up the pieces
You put back wrong

Yes, sometimes you're wrong
Yes, sometimes so am I
But this poem is yours, not mine

We are not playing cops and robbers now
These are real lives on the line
And you don't get to win all the time

Half a Heart

Oh kiss me softly
Kiss me kindly
Love me with gentle hands
I only have half a heart
But it's yours

I don't know how
to do this—
Don't know what love looks like
Up close

Is it a lovely, simple thing
Bright sunshine and the smell of grass?

Or is it something dark and mysterious
Still waters and writhing beasts?

I only have half a heart
Growth stunted by loneliness
In pivotal years
Not sure I know how to use it

But if I could love anyone
I know I'd love you

Be careful, be careful, please
I want to love you
If you'll only show me how

Don't Go

Alone in a ballgown
People smiling, laughing,
Rushing by.

Don't go.

Music plays, they dance away.

Don't go.
Don't go.

At parties like this
We stay out late,
But I can't come
Without a date.

Don't go.

Pink tulle surrounds me,
In a pastel cloud.
Please somebody show me
How not to be alone.

Come dance with me.

Don't go.

Monster

You be the Beauty
I'll be the Beast
Every day will be our wedding feast
And we'll all be dressed all in roses

You be the princess
I'll be the hag
And I'll kill all the monsters for you

I know that I'm one, too

If you want to transform me
I won't complain
Just let me stay
I may be a monster
But I'll make it worth your while
And we'll all be dressed in roses

Alone

These days I'm slipping back into old habits:
Crying myself to sleep for no reason
Sobbing in grocery store parking lots

I thought I was better
But then I thought a lot of things

I thought you would never leave
I thought things would never change
I thought I could handle this on my own
But I was wrong, oh I was wrong, and now I'm so alone

Spinning

I'm fine
      I'm fine
I have not
      (yet)
lost my mind
      I live on a merry go round
Spinning all the time
      (And the dizziness sets in)
My heart has stopped
      As have my lungs
          (I can hardly hold on)
My fingers are napping
      My head so light I could float
Like a birthday balloon
      Away
My world moves much too fast
      (And only ever in circles)
Lives outside blur and rush
      Away

I'm losing my grip
      Just stop for a minute
    (I'm so afraid)
   Just let me stay

Canoe

Bright yellow canoe
on the lake.
Water soft and smooth,
cool and clear.
Blue sky, blue water,
light bounces off waves.
Man in blue sweatshirt,
girl in red hat.
Push paddles through water,
glide across lake.
Paddles make whirlpools,
weeds drown
in miniature Charybdis.
Man steers around rock,
girl stares at fish
in the water below.
Cliffs rise above them,
tall, grey and orange.
No campground in sight,
paddlers weary.
Sun bright in their eyes,
canoe growing heavy,
holds three packs and a tent.
Mosquitoes buzz,
horseflies swarm.
Girl swats a bug,
man reaches for trail mix.
There's an island ahead.
Almost there now,
almost there.

Fall Apart

We fell together and fell apart
With the same unpracticed ease

We have been broken
In all the same ways
A matched set
Flawed, for a time, compatibly

But the cracks expanded
As cracks are wont to do
Until we stopped slotting together
And started aggravating each other's wounds

We became best friends overnight
Bonding over brokenness
We became nothing to each other
In the blink of an eye
And this is all I have to remember you by:
The scars we've always shared
And the new ones you gave me
When you fell away from my life

Apricots

Sometimes fruit rots
From the inside out
And that, I think,
Is what I have done
For I am lovely, lately
On the outside
But I can feel
The sticky sharp sweetness
Welling up
I am seldom bold
I do as I'm told
I am so sweet it sometimes
Hurts
But my sweetness has edges
That will slice you in half
And you can try to chew me up
But you will quickly spit me out
And the taste will never leave your mouth

Unless you want to be bitten back,
Don't bite the overripe fruit

Words I'm Not Saying

You could come back.

> (These are the stupid things I think
> Sleeping in a tent with the sound of rain
> Above me. A flash of lightning,
> And I'm floating on an inch of water,
> Half afraid I'll be swept away,
> And absurdly I think of you.)

You wouldn't have to take me camping.
It could be the way it was
When we were young

> (and we made
> Your couch a train and your father
> The mustachioed villain, unknowing,
> And the rain meant that we would go
> And save earthworms from the ditches
> And in my pockets there were always snakes,
> And we traded crabapples for garden bed rocks,
> One worthless item for another,)

And it was easy.

You could take me camping, if you like.
We wouldn't have to share a tent

> (But we could, if you like, and in the morning
> We could burn the pancakes together
> And search for blueberries)

And we could have fun again.

You wouldn't have to kiss me.
But you could come back.
Together we would be good campers.

Gardening

I used to believe in you
Grew up knowing you
Perfectly
You've become a stranger overnight
A man I don't remember
How to love

We used to garden together
Beans and tomatoes in neat little rows
And I saw our future
In those same clear lines

But somehow we shrunk
As the tomatoes grew

One morning I woke
To tiny bean flowers all in bloom
And when I went to tell you
I found you gone

Now there's seldom an answer
When I call your phone
So I eat all our veggies alone

Oz

The road is yellow, cobblestone,
And I think I've dropped you in the cracks
And I have removed my silver shoes.
Barefoot I might find you
And I am sick of blisters

You might have been made of glass
So clearly did I see your brain
Move through your head
Ideas rolling about like marbles
And I am so afraid that you will shatter

We have faced witches, you and I,
And together crossed the deadliest deserts
But now my chest is hollow
And the pumpkins in the fields rot
And I hope you are safe with your needle
Beneath all this straw

I would rather find you
And piece back together our patchwork love
But if you have flown away without me
Or if, found, you turn to china in my hands,
I will follow these bricks
To the fountain of Lethe
And forget you

I will turn my back on our city,
Green beneath the streetlights,
And catch a twister home.

For When I Don't Know How to Love

Things are strange, here in the silence between places we've been, and on winter nights I cannot sometimes tell between truth and fiction. We have not seen the sun in many days, but this may be better. In the sunlight all is clear, and I am running low on lies to tell.

My heart does not swell when I see you. Nothing swells. At times like this you are nothing to me. Sometimes, seeing you on the street, I fail to wave.

In conversation with Cupid I have confirmed this is not the romance you requested, but you have yet to lodge a formal complaint. His arrow hit and did not stick, for I am not made of things to be pierced. Something inside me is rusted and dusty and dead, but I am fond of you, I think.

You have not noticed, yet, that everything we are is only a symptom of storytelling. I do not know how to do these things sincerely, and most things live only in my head. Mostly I live only in my head, and there is seldom room for anyone else.

If I only had a heart, I think I would give it to you.

Changeling

I grew up sure I was a changeling
Swapped out at birth with some real child
Something false in a human's place

The question was never whether I was a person
But what, exactly, I might be instead

I might be some kind of monster
A demon, fairy child
Or I might be nothing but a stick or log
Enchanted to hold human shape

A question that haunted me for endless years—
Am I some wicked, broken creature
Doomed to be forever out of place
Or am I simply nothing alive at all?

Full grown I still don't have an answer
And I still sit up waiting most nights
For the fairies to take me away
Bring me somewhere I'll finally belong
Or revert me to an unliving log
But either way I'll be gone
Replaced with some other girl
Loveable and real and whole

Swan

I see the carcass of a swan on the side of the road
And think of you.
Do you remember when we fed the swans in the park?
It was the summer you had a buzz cut.
Do you remember those green branches hanging heavy
Above our heads?
Do you remember our reflections rippling in the pond
And the smell of bread?
And hay fever, laughing and sneezing
And the swans never came close enough?
The grass between our toes and coming home
Feet sticky with sap, and Mom yelling at us
For losing our shoes?
Do you remember the heat of the sun
And the bread dissolving in the water?

Swans should be soft and white but all I see is blood
And dirt and its neck is twisted.
Cars honk behind me. I taste feathers in my mouth
And wonder how something like that becomes
Roadkill.

Make a Wish

Click your heels

Make a wish, Make a wish, Make a wish

You play with chipped teacups
In hand-me-down shirts
And somebody somewhere
Has it worse
But this secondhand love still hurts.

The roads are all paved gray now
Gingham has gone out of style
And you don't know how
To be worthwhile
Make a wish, Make a wish, Make a wish

The world has grown up around you
But you are still a child
Who's forgotten how to smile
And you deserve so much more
Than this
And it won't come true
But it's something to do
Make a wish, Make a wish, Make a wish

Red Riding Cap

Your words sit heavy like stones in my stomach
And I cannot run to chase you down
I knew that one of us must be the Wolf
Big Bad

But I did not expect it to be me
I did not know what big teeth I had
Until they tore into your soul,
Bits catching between my braces,
I did not intend to gnaw on your heart
And devour you

But my eyes were not bigger to see you with,
My snout not enough to smell our decay
So leave me now while I am stilled with stones,
While the woodcutter savior looms

Run, Red Cap, run
Take yourself far away from me

Church

The cardboard taste of communion wafers
The bitterness of grape juice
Hitting recently-brushed teeth
A dozen voices happily raised
In an off-key chorus of praise
This is where I learned to love

Small, imperfect things

And no one understands now,
No one understands
How I've made my home
In the land of stained glass
When all my friends have long since moved past
Silly things like faith, like God, like family

But it's the only place I ever belonged
Where it wasn't a trial to play along
Where they took me just as I was

So even if I have to go alone
Every Sunday I'll still go home

They Say

I have ripped myself apart at the seams
With a box cutter—don't worry, it was clean
And sometimes life gets hard, they say
Hard.
Sometimes life is fucking torture
And you look in the mirror
And know you're too big
Because you can still see your face
And you can't find a diet
That makes your bones shrink
And there are voices in my head that scream
And everything will be okay, they say
Well maybe I don't want it to be
What dreams might I have
If my body remembered how to sleep
And what a drop in productivity
I am a mass of messy things
Anger, pain, anxiety, bits of blood and flesh
That never seem to go away
And just hold on, they say
And you don't answer because how can you
But it's just letting go
That I don't fucking know how to do
And I can't let it show
How some days I would if I could

Everything will be okay, they say

Lille Havfrue

This is what they don't tell you
About when the food refuses
To enter your mouth
Like two magnets with the same charge:
It takes your voice.
And every step you take
Is like walking on knives
As well as every word you say
You are always exhausted
And everything hurts.
When you try to sing it comes out hoarse
And off key because the emptiness
Has made your throat angry
And you don't know how to fill it up
When this body has ceased to be your own

Hole

Some days it still aches
The hole you left

You scooped yourself away
With a grapefruit spoon
Left me empty and alone and scraped raw

I used to think we were a pair
Now it seems we were two parts of the same whole
Seems I'm lost and incomplete without you

I remember sitting in the grass beside you
Weaving daisy chains while you read aloud
And the sun shone bright and it was easy

Now I pick daisies in that same field, strip it bare
To pluck their petals but no matter
What I do, how I count it out
You always love me not

Once I vowed never to hurt you
And didn't think
To extract the same promise for myself

You love me, you love me, you love me not
So I probe at the you shaped hole inside
Because it's the only thing you left me

From the Prince to Snow White: On the Subject of Your Death

Here is my mother
In the door to tell me again
"Bury the girl
She's starting to smell"
And there you are,
Perfect still like a china doll
In your glass coffin
And living like this with you
I have ignored the stench
Of rotten eggs

So this is not a story
Of life and apple
Pie
And I could blame my mother
For the truth
But I know that mirrors
Can be wrong
That some makeup is made
With poison
That Barbie waists are fine,
But Barbie doesn't breathe

I taught myself to kiss with pillows
Which never respond
So what did I expect from you
Whose body I stole in the woods?

I will buy you a nice headstone.

If you ever wake, please wake
For yourself or someone
Better than me.

Lord

I am not a woman, but a worm
So much less than what you made me
I am the thing that lives beneath the dust

Lord,
Deliver me to ninth grade biology
Where they will pull me apart
Find dirt and feces
Let them throw pins and darts
At my small waxen heart

Lord I don't know how to feel a thing
Lord worms dry up so fast
But you pour the water to keep me alive

Lord, you died, you died
And left me nothing, only me

Lord stay with me or take me home
Don't leave me in the dust alone

Merry Go Round

We used to have a merry go round
        At the bottom of the hill behind the park
Where our dads played softball on
                            Thursdays
        I used to dream about that merry go round
I used to think
        If I could run fast enough
              If I could push hard enough
                  If I built enough momentum
              Before I jumped
        Maybe
Maybe I could fly
        Maybe it could spin me off the ground
              And bring me to a better world

        They removed it last summer
And put in a swing set

        They told the newspapers it wasn't safe.

They didn't tell how everyone's laugh
        Was a song when we spun
            How the sky went silver
The smell of lilacs
        The taste of rain
            And the soft loose dirt that swirled around
        In the air
            Packed hard beneath our feet
How the dizzy giddy soaring spinning
            Was almost magic

They didn't tell the newspapers that.

I Miss You But I Don't Want You Back

I miss the way you smile
How your eyes squeeze shut
And one side of your mouth
Comes up a little higher

I miss talking through the bathroom door
Taking turns getting ready in the morning

The stupid, little things
Your tangled hair and how you sing off key
The shared books on our shelf
The movies we convinced each other to watch

I miss how things were when things were good
I miss you
But I don't want you back
And I hate you for becoming
A different kind of person
Hate you for giving me mixed feelings
How I cry for the loss of you
Even as I run away

I don't miss the sound of your raised voice
The stupid fights that became the only conversation
We ever had
The sneaking, snide remarks
I didn't understand
I don't miss the days I stayed out late
Hoping you would be asleep
Left in the morning before you woke up
Don't miss the way I devoted free hours
To avoiding your aimless anger

I miss you but I don't want you back

Matching Scars

I wish I could say I love you
And have it be fully true
I know I once said I always would
But I hope you know I would have loved you still
If you hadn't changed into someone I barely knew

I hope you know I forget not to count you
Some nights when I set the table
I hope you know all the snowmen I make
I still give them your favorite names

I hope the person you used to be
Still lives somewhere inside you
I hope that person still loves the person I used to be
I hope you still think of me
When our favorite stars peak out through the trees

I hope whoever you are
Who I was is still branded on your heart
I wish for us, now grown apart
An eternity of matching scars